SPORADIC TROUBLESHOOTING

D1501664

SPORADIC TROUBLESHOOTING

CLARENCE MAJOR

poems

Louisiana State University Press *Baton Rouge*

Published by Louisiana State University Press
lsupress.org

Copyright © 2022 by Clarence Major
All rights reserved. Except in the case of brief quotations used in articles or reviews,
no part of this publication may be reproduced or transmitted in any format or by any
means without written permission of Louisiana State University Press.

LSU Press Paperback Original

Designer: Michelle A. Neustrom
Typeface: Sentinel

Cover image: *Family Togetherness,* 1976, by Clarence Major

Grateful acknowledgment is extended to the following journals and magazine in
which some of these poems originally appeared:

"The Metropolitan Museum of Art," "Caught by Light," "Gravity and Weight," "The
Little Cascades," and "Not Lately": *The American Scholar Quarterly;* "Hair": *Best
American Poetry* and *The New Yorker;* "Territorial Claims": *Callaloo;* "The Cycle":
Catamaran Magazine; "At the Market," "Irish Nell," "Slow Dance," and "The Trip":
The Chicago Quarterly Review; "Sardines": *Cutthroat: A Journal of the Arts;* "Las
Vegas Strip": *Konch Magazine;* "Mt. Rushmore" and "Supply and Demand": *The New
Yorker;* "He Said" and "Not Naming": *Oversound;* "Dangerous Creatures": *Stone,
River, Sky: An Anthology of Georgia Poems;* "The Grand Canyon," "Brooklyn Bridge,"
and "Statue of Liberty": *Taint Taint Taint;* and "In *Night of the Iguana* (1964)":
World Poetry of the 21st Century.

Library of Congress Cataloging-in-Publication Data

Names: Major, Clarence, author.
Title: Sporadic troubleshooting : poems / Clarence Major.
Description: Baton Rouge : Louisiana State University Press, [2022]
Identifiers: LCCN 2021030824 (print) | LCCN 2021030825 (ebook) |
   ISBN 978-0-8071-7610-8 (paperback) | ISBN 978-0-8071-7749-5 (PDF) |
   ISBN 978-0-8071-7750-1 (epub)
Subjects: LCGFT: Poetry.
Classification: LCC PS3563.A39 S66 2022 (print) | LCC PS3563.A39 (ebook) |
   DDC 811/.54—dc23
LC record available at https://lccn.loc.gov/2021030824
LC ebook record available at https://lccn.loc.gov/2021030825

CONTENTS

SPORADIC TROUBLESHOOTING

Sporadic Troubleshooting

Castor wants to know
which is his father—
a swan or a king.
Updating the story
has an odd effect on its truth.
The swan wants to know
a few things of his own.
The melting of resistance
is a well-kept secret.

Leda loves novelty. Obviously!
The king loves Sparta.
What are these missteps
ostensibly passing for seduction?
Most of us love the novelty of it.
We also love trustworthy companions.

There are some clues
in any opera or comic strip.
But what is the hidden purpose
of delight?
A friend is having an affair
with a rich, gorgeous woman
called Leda.
In full atonement
there is no turning back.

I learn a lot
on the elevated platform
waiting for the train.

Even when
there is a superb performance
the end is always the same.

The boy works in a hotel
where he meets rich women
on vacation.

Nothing here is divinely appointed.
But certain things can be evoked
and surpassed.
It is a whole distant world
full of fascinating mystery.
The king has oddly little effect
on the outcome.
Leda will eventually leave
her husband
and marry her lover.

A pagoda on the distant shore
glows like a jaunty diamond.

The boy sprays breath spray
in his mouth
before going up to the rooms.
We all have a part
in separating purity
from the perverse.
The king is already the dupe.

But he keeps jaguars and tigers
by his side.
We all know Leda's trips
to the woods are not to bird-watch.
The underlying menace
never leaves the place.
Once I went with her
just to see what would happen.

I cherish the sound of her voice.
One libretto in the afternoon
seems to do the trick.

I learn a lot
from this experience
about sympathy and symmetry.
Not surprisingly, it all adds up.
Everything is significant.

Sardines

Lower East Side, mid-1960s

On weekends
Ray always came back drunk.
His key fumbling in the lock.
He would give up
and sink to the floor.
I'd open the door,
pick him up and pull him inside.
Often beaten up and robbed
Ray came back crawling.
I walked the streets
to give him some privacy.
I was doing research
on the future of the human race.
I sat in Jimmy's
and made one beer last for hours.
The Lower East Side
was becoming the East Village.
The perfect place
to research the future
of the human race.
I lived on sardines
and saltine crackers.
With sardine-breath,
I hung out in Tompkins Square Park
among acidheads and LSD-heads,
among hippies and Flowers Children.
Hippies playing bongo drums
entertaining the Flower Children.
The smell of marijuana
filling the air and the trees.
Middle-class kids from Long Island
shacked up in flophouses.
Where better to research

the future of the human race?
Walking 5th and 14th
and Houston and Broadway,
I was deep in my research
on the future of the human race.
I wandered down into Chinatown
and across the Brooklyn Bridge.
Looking for clues
to the future of the human race.
Everywhere I found evidence
of a future for the human race.
Searching, I walked
the whole seventy-nine square miles.
Saturday-night music on the streets
and people dancing at The Cave.
I researched it all
for the future of the human race.
For twenty cents, I rode
the first air-conditioned subway.
Evidence of progress
for the human race.
I rode Uptown
and walked the streets of Harlem
documenting
the future of the human race.
In Midtown, I loved
the cool solitude of art museums.
Keeping in touch with creativity
for the future of the human race.
In Washington Square Park,
I sat on the fountain and took notes
for the future of the human race.

A Basket of Apples

She didn't have her teeth in
when they took the snapshot.
Said her mouth had changed
and the dentures now hurt.

Take away her wool coat
and give her summer.
Take away her frown
and add people to the balcony.
Take away the houses behind her;
add a sunny hillside of sunflowers.

She's wearing those heavy earrings.
They've given her elongated earlobes.

Take away her tears
and her tragic memories.
Give her a basket of apples.
Place them on her arm.
If that's not possible
give her back her small ears.

The Seven-Headed Dragon

A girl was shivering
in the downpour.

We gathered
as if before the alchemist.
Seasonal delicacies were served.

But what did David do
with the head of Goliath?

Charitable workers
claimed the Seven Acts of Mercy.
Seven sections of attendees
struggled for agreement.
Some proposed seven things.
Some proposed starting over.
Some of us sat on the curb
and sulked, losing our purpose.

I became wild-eyed Caravaggio
as Bacchus up to no good,
holding a bunch of white grapes.

Seven colleagues
in joisting armor
entered the tournament.

A fake-Durer,
as a well-hung melancholic,
posed for pictures.

By nightfall
torrential rains
ended our efforts.

Finally, Hercules
at the crossroads.
Armed Minerva
pulling the Centaur by his hair!
He was miserable.
She was sad. I got ready
for my next performance.

Supply and Demand

As a dishwasher
in a restaurant
I lasted only three hours.
It was a dubious role at best.
The dirty dishes kept coming
faster than I could produce clean ones.
But I could play the piano
for hours and hours,
snake across the floor
on my belly
all afternoon into the night.
As Hercules
I lifted Antaeus from the earth,
robbing him of his strength.
Always happy,
I could walk around the block
on my hands.
In a fanciful costume,
I played the joker.
With a thirty-pound sack of rice
on my head, all day,
I danced
on a stone balustrade
without falling off.
From sunup to sundown,
week after week
I was a whole amusement park
unto myself.
I was on top of contingencies.
I defended victims of foolishness
and porous people.
I campaigned for weeks
against the greedy.
I deconstructed ancestral suffering.

I gave comfort to the feeble
and the needy.
I made marionettes dance for kids.
I played marbles with the best
and the worst.
But as a dishwasher
I lasted only three hours.

Rococo

Shooting through the underground
I'm on my way
to the outermost limits
of Brooklyn
to teach a class.

The train is like an enclosed fortress
a space severely cropped,
a space of wacky geometric patterns.

Some people reading
some gazing off into eternity,
a few napping.

It's an allegory of gestural brushwork.
Aggressively hideous,
one guy crudely mocking everybody,
another with delicate fingers
picking pockets.
A scoundrel roaming about
looking for trouble.
Two girls in jeans
frolicking through.

I'm looking up into the cosmos,
wondering how the people
up in the space station are doing.

Territorial Claims

While walking a narrow path
high above Boulder,
looking for a place to rest,
I paused at a large rock
alongside a diverging path
and saw, standing on a rock
(of grays and greens—
the same as her own colors),
a pregnant lizard, a skink
standing high,
careful to keep her belly lifted
from her perch,
the hot surface,
while she, weary of trouble,
watched me coolly
calculating my next move,
determined
to protect her inner bubble,
brave enough to go to war
with me, if necessary.
So, I moved off the path
far from her,
making a large circle,
concluding it,
up beyond her rock
and again, took up my search
for a place I could claim my own.

Recto! Verso!

Homer's Odyssey: slave traders
throwing sick bodies overboard.
Your eye produces a tear.

You touch the starter
before anything happens.
One starts with an idea
or a good sentence.

Apollo with his bow
and arrow ready . . .
Diana seated on a rock
gazing into the distance.

1490: fishermen deciding
to search Lake Constance.
They find the body of a boy.
Deliverance!

Heraclitus decided fate was real.
He called it geography.

There were urban
and civic amenities too.
Calligraphy was already in use.

Madonna sat on the crescent moon!
Saint Michael got results too.
The dragon lay at his feet.

Did you ever notice
how goofy Durer's dragons are?
And who can argue
with The Whore of Babylon?

Upinhere

Upinhere is a place of high status;
a place of privacy and comfort.

Mother said
I don't want any foolishness
up in here. No liquor!
No lunatics, no tricks,
nobody kicking and screaming.
No lying, no fighting,
no cussing and drooling.
No malice, no crimes,
no late nights, no drugs.

No bad manners period,
up in here.

Once when we left
the door opened
swallows flew up in here.

When the floor moved
we knew it was an earthquake.
Our confidence up in here
was badly shaken.

We endured early *lights out*
up in here and catfights too.

We survived *the sweet here after,*
lost car keys and endured nasty chitchats.

We wore out the checkerboard.
Chess pieces were lost up in here.

We lived with a thin veneer
on everything everywhere up in here.

We played harmonicas
all night up in here.
Harp all morning
and banjo all afternoon.

Most of all we cherished
our little things of comfort:
bottles, goblets,
carafes, pitchers, sugar bowls.
A lovely daguerreotype
of grandfather wearing a bowtie.
We loved his copper pots,
his turnip peeler, his pepperbox.

Dreamy-eyed, effortlessly,
sister played the piano.
Played it from sunrise to sunset.
Then she got married up in here.

But my gaze stayed fixed
on the square of sunlight high
up on the wall way up in there.

The Ring and the Nest

The bird's nest
beneath the seats.

I'm told
people don't dance in the ring.
But sometimes what happens
looks like a dance.

This time
the man is humiliated,
not the animal.

The band plays loudly.

A boy climbs the wall
to escape the horns.

At the gun blast,
in a mosaic of colors,
birds suddenly fly up
from the arena.
It's like
applying a thin layer
then dragging an impasto
across it.

Not surprisingly
we are not having fun.

Before they bring out the bulls
they torture them.

Fortunately
they can't catch the birds.
What's with people?

Longevity

Thirty years from now:
She is in her backyard
in a plastic lawn chair.
He is dead.
She has in her hands his *Complete Poems*.

She turns the pages,
reading slowly
(slowly, like people used to read).

She comes to that delightful poem,
her favorite poem in the book.
She is stunned by its symmetry,
by its climate, by its daylight.

She is amazed by its tunnels,
its muscle, its tambourines, its guitars!
She is pleased by the brushwork of its surface.
She is charmed by its lovely antlers.

She is awakened by its bells
and by the silent film of its alter ego.
She is lured by its flora and fauna,
by its rivers and streams.

She wakes at three in the morning
and reads it again and again.
This time she reads deeper
into its degrees of dark forest.
She is amazed by the specter
of its desert and dense jungle.

She reads it every day
for three months, swimming in its seas.

Each time she finds new adventures
in its foothills and underbrush.
She finds snowed-in mountaintops
and a glowing Sphinx!
She finds an array of winds
and clouds and rainbows.
She finds a sequence of sleet and snow
on mountain peaks.

She finds Josephine Baker
moving with ease
through Nazi checkpoints.
And finally:
She returns to her chair
in the yard
to write her own poem.

He Said

He said
he could be happy anywhere
because
somewhere at sometime
a long stretch
of poppies are blooming.
In lilac season
the sweet smell fills the ar.
Marigolds under the sun
are at their brightest.
In Australia the great myrtles
are standing tall.
In western China, he said,
the cherry trees are in bloom.
With its scaly bark
the white oak
of Quebec is sparkling.
Junipers, silver furs,
beech and lime
are having their turn.
The camellias of the evergreen
are glowing red in sunlight.
He praised forget-me-nots
in upper windows!
The lilies and the larkspur,
he said, are blooming wild.
And he praised the poor
persimmon tree too
with its possum wood—
it and all the rest
springing from the blood
and tears of the human earth.

Dangerous Creatures

Lovely Simonetta
squeezing milk from her nipple.

See the seven-headed dragon.
And here comes the angel
with the key to the abyss.

And what of that thing
that intoxicates officials.
That monstrous craving
for more and more ...

The alchemist
in search of the philosopher's stone.
I'm with you, Abigail!
They are dangerous creatures.
They say a glass of water
and a piece of bread!
Then go to bed.

Devil if they know what to do!
They think it may be
the great enigma.

No sympathy, no empathy.
The emptiness
is as heavy as the fullness.

A cup of tea!
And what's on the plate?
The riddle of the Sphinx.
Dirty dishes in the sink.

Very desperate people
lined up in an alley.
I don't rally
and I don't believe in fate.

In *Night of The Iguana* (1964)

Puerto Vallarta, 1968

Shannon drives the tour bus
down the hill
and on by my apartment
(my apartment
four years later)
on the corner of Hidalgo
at the bottom of the hill
and he turns the corner
going alongside the creek
passing the women
scrubbing clothes on the rocks
and goes on out of town
to Maxine's.
I climb the hill
to Maxine's hotel.
Charlotte no longer there.
Along with his wheelchair,
the body of Hannah's grandfather
Cyril no longer there.
In town the shop windows
displaying autographed pictures
of Ava and Richard.
My landlady asks me to stay
and manage the building.
Maxine makes Shannon the same offer.
He accepts. I don't.

Mostly Water

It's on stilts!
Carrying pipes and tubes.
Blushing rivulets
rushing through pipes.
It spends its life
in a cinematic
and ambiguous atmosphere.

Amulets on the ankles
jangle like cowbells.
It is a vaporous field
of emotion in motion.

It daydreams
at the slow swirling edge
of the sea.

Surely that familiar place
causes no anxiety.
What of size and symmetry
of this tenement of clay?
A storehouse of bones
and shreds.

The bed
must also contain the girl
with the cello.
Her music is necessary.
She's on the deck
beneath two balloons
full of water.

They are suspended
from a chandelier.
The chandelier gently moving
in the breeze.
Soon she and the cello
will be drenched.
But ah! Typical
of this ongoing conundrum.

Charity

Putting things out
for charity pickup:

The charity truck will come
and the driver will inspect
the things as they warm
in midmorning sunlight.

In a melancholy blur,
twenty minutes later,
I think, wait a minute.

But
why do we want our stuff back;
minutes after we surrender it.
How many scintillating minutes
in a lifetime of giving
and repossessing?
Propensity speaks
unmistakably.
It's ludicrous but true.

So, I go back out
to the curb
and bring my things back
inside.
Endurance is important,
not the things we keep
or surrender.

Exacerbated by boundaries,
demarcations placed around me,
I struggle
against my trappings.

When the dark cloak
of night arrives
and the lines are drawn
fluidly around me,
even my dilemma
will be pointless.

The chessboard—
both grim and joyous as a Giotto—
is stacked against a total win
and a total loss.

Not Lately

Anne Boleyn
said the king was good to her.
She was promoted
more than once.
Then the final promotion.

But I never thought progress
had anything do with death.
On second thought
maybe it does.
Somehow death turns out
to be the point.

Like that time in Argentina:
everything was absolute—yet fluid.
Like religion.
Like the birth of a new idea.

But I say
consider the alternative.
You can live *and* kill the idea.
Kill it with a stick.
Get the picture?
Think of it as a snake
about to strike.
Whack!
Right across the head!
You *can* kill a snake.
You are acting in self-defense.

And don't worry.
They don't burn people
at the stake anymore.
At least not lately.

Not Naming

Something large
as the battle of sea gods.

I feel it
but refuse to name it.
Nameless
it remains large.

Given a name it is reduced
to a word, a name, an idea.

The hurdy-gurdy man
with rheumatism
playing classical tunes.
See what I mean?
"Play that tune slowly
hurdy-gurdy man!"

Two mules stopping
because a wheel comes off
the wagon.
See—there it is again!

Two boys whitewashing
the footbridge across the creek!
But where is the largeness?

Whitman says, "Sing the great oak,
sing the flowing creek."

And I help repair the wagon.
I tip the hurdy-gurdy man.

I cross the bridge
to visit the cemetery
to see the large headstone.

But next time
give me something large
as the battle of sea gods.

My Sister's Lungs

Her lungs
black with smoke damage.
She notoriously refused to change.
Smoked from age fifteen
to seventy-one.

Inherited good taste
but made bad decisions.
None of us had a unique claim
on the truth of it.
From the hospice
she called the funeral home.

Her life was hung
in pipe-and-flange armature.

We were on a makeshift timetable,
waiting for the end.

She worked a boring job
never gave up and always gave.

On vacation
she raged and gambled.
Everything about her
was full-scale.

She said,
"I don't want my casket opened."

She never discovered the delights
of a quiet life.
Relatives, full of remembrance,
opened it anyway.

At the end pain was swallowing her body.
Even as she lay dying
the nurse refused her pain pills.
No savior came
handing out samples of goodness.

Outside and Inside the Castle

We park the car
and approach the castle.

Out beyond the grounds:
the vineyard—neatly manicured
rows of grape vines
plump with green grapes.
Nearby, black goats
and white sheep grazing together
on the grassy grounds.
Geese and ducks busy
scratching around the castle.

Sleepy guards patrolling,
as though it were a fortress,
patrolling with antique rifles grown heavy.
We walk the cobbled passageways
and alleyways,
first one way then back,
then around and back again.

We go inside.
In the great long social room
a stone floor of earth colors.
A long dining table of ancient oak,
made for royalty and polite chatter.

Chairs tucked to it, oak and empty,
fifty on each side, standing like sentries.
On the walls, silent paintings
in red gold and blue
paintings of ancient holiness,
a world long gone, yet still here.

Up higher and higher
daylight pouring down
through stained-glass windows.
Six on either side;
colors yellow, red, blue, gold,
and a bluer blue.

The ceiling, a network of dark oak
crossbeams; ancient hardwood.

Now we go to the basement.
Down here hundreds of barrels
of wine sleeping
in cool fermenting contentment.
Tuscan wines—
We sample the Merlot!
The Cabernet,
the Pinot Grigio!
The Pinot Bianco!

Now we've worked up an appetite.
Time to find a good restaurant.

Horrid Light

Maybe the sagging gate
was once straight.
I don't know.
Everybody out here
talked at once.

But two guys inside
said the architectural effect
was not convincing.

And why was the parrot
a serious part of the conversation?

In early 1936 ownership changed hands.

Everybody said it was completely legal.
Of course, they all blamed me.
Although I wasn't born yet,
I accepted blame anyway.

It was better
to do the honorable thing.
I wasn't trying to be a martyr.
I was just trying
to avoid an argument.

In the dream
I was handed a pass—but to what . . . ?
I say answer to the charges—
no matter the nature.
Besides, the people in back
could hardly control their killer dog.

And Milton said Nature is not to blame.
Neglect is the obvious
opposite of this dilemma.
Maybe the sagging gate
was once very straight.

Before all of this happened
ceremonies were private.
Swords, crowns, titles.
Deeds! Decrees!
Ideas in the horrid light
of too much power.

Music Hall

We were neighbors then.
We all hung out together
at the bar and in the cafes.
Remember when
she was a little girl?

Butterflies in a jar.
A girl playing cops and robbers
with the boys.
And when necessary
babysitting one of them.

He was her toy!
She's now dancing
to piano music in a music hall.
Dance, Simone, dance!
She dances in Paris, in Berlin, in Venice.

The devil doesn't have all the good tunes.
For her piano music
is love and a treat.
Sweet concord!
Sweet accordione!

Sweet guitar!
But the devil, she says, keeps busy.
And her friend Barbara needs a new way
to play yet another fallen female.

Gravity and Weight

The suspension rings
and the butterfly pumps
were in good working order.
All the mortise joints and the pulleys
and pistons were working properly.
These things had already passed inspection.
Surely the trap door below
had passed inspection too.
We knew something down there
was breathing, breathing heavily.
The policemen were responding
to another false alarm.
On the road
runners kept passing by.
Shadows got longer and longer.
By now all the pulleys,
strung from fruit trees
in the front yard, were broken.
Nobody remembered
what they were for,
but the water-mill wheel
was still working.
The priest still stopped by
to see if the boys
working in the kitchen,
were behaving themselves.
One of the boys had broken
the chocolate grinder
but nobody cared.
We all ate chocolate
straight from the sacks.

At night in the yard
we watched the Milky Way
twinkling and glowing.
It was a hell of a lot of fun.

Two Egrets

Flapping and struggling
the female is stuck,
her neck under his wing.
It's breeding season
for the monogamous.
I step out into the pond
and wade out to them.
She's quacking and calling.
Nearby
geese and ducks watching.
I gently work
neck and wing loose,
one from the other.
I pull the female up
onto the embankment.
Serrated beak stretching
in fearful silence.
She flaps about,
her massive wingspread
giving her balance.
Gaining it, without drama,
she wobbles a bit.
I redirect her to her mate.
Free now, they sail off together.

The Party

Rutting,
we wanted something bright.
It was spring where all the bells ring
at the same time
under a crayon rainbow.
Gathering gaily
in an open-air cabaret.
No lost wages
or fear of bankruptcy.
We were all intoxicated
with expectation.
Beyond the chatter,
goldfinches in their cages
singing up a storm.
How desperately we need each other.
It's enticing to think
that none of it was as I remember.
The party was an allegory
of small gestures.
We had a corrosive appetite
for cornered delusions.
I was Sisyphus
pushing a boulder
up an impossible hill.
The flamboyant giggles
were ludicrous.
The gathering
was a glowing snapshot
I keep at the back of a scrapbook.
It brings back those wondrous times!

Nate's Dungeon

The cross
was still a viable option.

They hung the first man
who dared to cross the line.

The old ballads got it right.

Consider rules
for the regulation of swearing.
That wooden collar
restricting breathing.

Cyclone Carry
promising to give them hell
when she got out.

And the rich too delicate,
too refined to do time.

Even a "Boo!" in the dark
was too much.

It's not moral to break the poor,
nor is it ethical or aesthetic,
yet it goes on unstopping.

Be glad the gallows and the gibbet
are gone.
It's enough that life itself
is parasitic!

Faith of the Protagonist

You are in your armchair
reading the newspaper.

You are now at the window
waiting for three o'clock.

Which part of you is the protagonist,
which the supporting actor?
When will you become modern?

You are fishing at the estate creek.
You see yourself
headed for a panoramic vista
of modernity in a series of trick mirrors.
And there is no shortcut
to getting there or getting out.

Under a cloudy sky
the railway stretches
into a distant landscape.

Because you remember what happed there
the backyard stairway
to the second floor
makes your heart ache.

The afternoon sunlight
turns it to a glowing altar
with no worshippers.

Though rich,
you are wearing the blue smock
of modest labor.

You gaze into the iron
of an unknown stratum
of modernity becoming obsolete as it arrives.

The iron girders
of your life transfix you

yet up ahead the earth curves away and up
into an unknown distance you can't see.

You have a penchant
for surviving the Sorrow.

Tomorrow the new tapestries
will reflect the spatial and the temporal.
Then you will be free,
free to put *being modern* behind you.

At the Rink

My memory of my rink effort
is like a silent film.
A silent film with scratch marks,
blotches and blacked-out areas.

Largesse of spirit,
my date grabbed me.
She held me up.

I tried to skate
as I had skated long ago
with skill and dash.
But that was sidewalk-skating.
A different skill!
Now, on this smooth surface,
I kept stumbling,
slipping and sliding.

No alter ego to take my place,
I turned the color of turquoise.
Where was my doppelgänger
to save me from this humiliation?

Out of breath,
on the notion I choked
on scrambled embarrassment.

Soon, my date set out
to skate on her own.
I'd hit a bump in the road
and all my tires were flat.

I stumbled off the rink
and sat on a bench, mortified.
I immediately made plans
to become a monk.

Folly

Much of it was unimaginable.
Some bought flowers
from the vendor on the way in.
Henry called them golden kisses.
Others brought other flowers:
Roses! Daffodils! Dandelions! Petunias! Lilacs!

Some were like proverbs.
Others like steamboats.
Steamboats with steam floating above!
Out in the lobby
it was clear
the dunce had a good memory.
He remembered
to line the flowerpots with rocks.
The charmer said get used to it
everything takes forever.

A blossom here, a blossom there.
No relief from the glitter
of swords in sunlight.
Men aggressively out
to kill each other.
The dark hidden flowerless lives
of workers bent along the docks.

One owned a chimp as a hobby.
They were the subjects of journalists.
Dense chatter
of the book party spilling into the lobby!
All absurd beyond belief.
But what did you expect?

Bricklayers

When I'm stuck,
when I'm blocked,
I forget transparency.
I go for the covert operation.
It gives me dreamtime
on double time.

Often the retention storehouse
down there is closed off.
Under cover,
I beseech the bricklayers.
But it's hard
to get their attention.

I pretend I don't seek it.
I sneak down to see
what the hell's going on.
If I'm quick,
I can grab one by the scruff.
Hold on like light to lightning.
Close the trap door
so he can't jump back in the hole.
That's how I get what I need. It works.

Mermaid

We're on the terrace.
Crowd in the plaza cheering.
We don't buy the nazioni line.
We like the cello player though.
The wind is strong up here.
Angelina holds onto her big straw hat.
She says
they're cheering a hoi polloi ignoramus.

But now
the mermaid has come
out of the sea.
Soon the plaza will be empty
and soaked.
There are days
when we welcome a storm.

On Sight

. . . So, we looked at other things—
The sky. Hiking trails. Jackets. Rings.
The density of the forest. A Victorian spoon.
Shoes. Backpacks. Boots. Trees. Dog collars.
Earphones. Nametags. Fallen shingles.

For a long time
we thought the moon *was* a wheel of cheese.
We learned
that a man on his knees
was not necessarily praying.
Many were broken by life.

Beneath this tinsel
was *another* tinsel.

A patch over one eye.
All we could think of
was the eye beneath the patch.
We want to know the unknown.

Village Festival

Yes, there were revelers
throwing pretzels.
Yes, it was like a generic allusion
to jousting.
Yes, it was like a village kermis.
Yes, some of us were lured by bait.
Yes, one guy ate his way
to the next village; arriving late.
Yes, two cupids fought
over a rose.
Yes, there were dogs
squabbling over a bone.
Yes, there were pomposities.
There was parody too.
Yes, Charles the First escaped
into the hands of guards.
Yes, like Brueghel,
I was there disguised
as a country bumpkin.

Deep Seated

Deep seated
like the tongue in the throat
like grains in wood,
like imp in impish
Like red dye
in the wings of an insect

Restrained
Indelible like light green
in deep green

Grace has an interest in life,
deep life

Ingrained
I can almost see it
with wings flying above danger
It flows extensively
with an extended sense
of flowing,
as though
it has a separate existence
so strong it might outlive us,
it will outdo us

Hair

In the old days
hair was magical.
If hair was cut
you had to make sure it didn't end up
in the wrong hands.

Bad people could mix it
with, say, the spit of a frog.
Or mix it with the urine of a rat!
And certain words
might be spoken.
Then horrible things
might happen to you.

A woman with a husband
in the navy
could not comb her hair after dark.
His ship might go down.

But good things
could happen, too.
My grandmother
threw a lock of her hair
into the fireplace.
It burned brightly.
That is why she lived
to be a hundred and one.

My uncle had red hair.
One day it started falling out.
A few days later
his infant son died.

Some women let their hair grow long.
If it fell below the knees
that meant
they would never find a husband.

Braiding hair into cornrows
was a safety measure.
It would keep hair
from falling out.

My aunt dropped a hairpin.
It meant somebody
was talking about her.

Birds gathered human hair
to build their nests.
They wove it round sticks.
And nothing happened to the birds.

They were lucky.
But people?

The Little Cascades

An unimpeded stream
pours swiftly down effusively
through rock into an indolent creek,
then shifts softly to floating,
then back to indolence,
disturbing
the creek's tendency to stagnate.
At any rate a dubious journey.
Always in transition,
always embellishing,
this little place of rock,
moss, and water
and dappled tree bark.
A vaporous mist rising
from the creek.
It mirrors, in its small way,
the mutable clouds
floating above;
and I stand here on vacation
marveling
at the system
of communication
between creek and sky,
between tree and water,
between rock and moss,
between me and it.

Red Skies

Then always turned out to be *now*
with or without suspicion

He stayed inside
Blind and wore a little tight suit

People on the balcony waiting
for the currency exchange to open

Flood insurance
but it didn't mean anything
They paid by the week

You ask
who are those men in the yard?
Dressed in work clothes
and bibbed caps
Trees leaning over
because of the gale
Skies scorched red
A promise of more trouble
and it's already here

Go Figure

Am I ever prepared
for anything?

There is a rift in the future.
Who will implement a noble idea?
What is the angle
of contingency?

The dictionary says: "anticipate"
means to "be prepared for";
secondary meaning:
to "look forward to."

There are resources
but can I depend on them?

I return happily
to the known tradition.

That is my best chance
for navigating
these unknown waters
but don't call me traditional.

Caught by Light

I wander among birch
to see fallen leaves of many colors.
I climb a hill
with a sprinkle of hillside flowers.
I reflect to collect myself
and down by the river green
a white stucco at river's edge
covered with ivy
from ground to roof
and down the other side;
and from inside,
I hear TV news of war
tanks and city banks
going broke,
wrongdoings
with no good defense,
murder and rare snakebites
a thief caught
by light climbing a fence.

Between Love and Like

We were talking
about what I felt for her.
I said it's somewhere
between "love" and "like."

She said like Bogart
in *Casablanca* to Bacall!
Remember? He raises his glass
and says, "Here's looking at your kid."

Or you want to kiss my hand?
As if my hand wrote *Ulysses*!
But that's as far as you want to go.
To you, I am like integrity,
patriotism and loyalty.

I'm a rose without a thorn.
I'm like great art in the museum.
But the sign says Do Not Touch.

I'm like good music.
Nice to listen to.
I said, Yes,
that's exactly what I feel.
But it wasn't!

Like Money

You grew into it.
It felt like artificial respiration.
It was the kind of activity
that came to obsess you.

But you took the bull
by the ear with a death knell ringing.

If you were seventeen
you thought about it all the time.

Tallulah Bankhead
wasn't going to get there by five.
She said so.

Baudelaire saw it
in the lyricism of the masses.
If only you had read
The songs of Solomon out loud.

By twenty-one
you were already
over the bluff
crossing the boulder.

At breakneck speed
and in no time flat
you were already
going down the other side.

Irreversible

By the coffee shop
the tribal god stands,
grand, erect, mute, wooden.
He represents safe passage
over water—rough rapids!

The footpath runs diagonal
to the bridge.
Local women in its shade
fanning themselves.

Then
there is the Monarch Butterfly.
He lands weightlessly on the bridge,
folding and unfolding
those lovely decorated wings.

Madame says,
"You should read
that Polynesian novel.
It has butterflies
and lots of local women."

Tomato

I could welcome one,
a perfect one, so red, so smooth.
At the checkout counter,
the clerk says
"They move away, or they pass away."
And TJ in Taos
with the mountains
moving in, moving in;
at one with the universe
and the mountains moving in.
It's November and
I can't find a good tomato anywhere.
But the sky is blue and clear
and the golden-yellow leaves
(as I see them
through the window now)
are turning rusty red
and a brighter yellow.
And I'm grateful,
grateful for the colors,
grateful for the seasons.

Prints

Not *Indian*—
that was an error: *Aborigine.*

I arrived early
to photograph a family of thirty.

I stood beneath scrub pine
for shadow, under overcast sky.

They were standing on earth
of snow pellets,
the rest of winter stuff.
I clicked and clicked and clicked.

Later together we broke bread,
dipping it in steaming stew.

They showed me sacred places,
sacred symbols carved in rock,
sacred ancestors stored in memory.

We stood outside their home,
a shack of plywood
with a metal roof.
We talked
using both languages.

It was late
when I waved goodbye
and drove away—never to forget.

September

Left-handed,
the English he learned
was right-handed.
Out on the plains,
Heaven and John Keats.
His superstitions
were no worse than ours.
A wolf's howl
raising a human soul.
Mountain lions coming down,
thirsty and hungry.
Explain any of this
to the seekers of the yellow rock.
At night, beseeched
we heard nightingales all night.
Trying to mediate,
Chief's brother-in-law
stood making his speech.
We made peace
with the miners from Ludlow.
Fiona and Sharp by day
finally made up and ate together.
By then something good
would have to happen.
That was one way
that year we avoided war.
Keeping peace is a struggle.

Abstract Expressionism

In the bar
the old gas stove burning coal.
She says,
Don't say barmaid, say bartender!

Just then
one of the soldiers takes her hand.
Tenderly,
he dances her out onto the floor.

They swirl around
and around.

Still carrying her tray
she never spills a drop.

Arithmetic

I first sensed it
while up in a fig tree.

Blue jays
hopping from limb to limb.

But it was the summer leaves
rustling all around me.

The red-chested robins
calling out warnings.

The *swoosh* of cars going by.

In church the pretty girl
at the piano.

Lil playing the piano
was Gauguin's boys wrestling.

Rossini's laundry list
hung out to dry.

And Liszt opening the lid
to let the sound out.

Thirst

I park my car
in front of the ranger's house.
I stand on an outcropping
of rock.

I lean out,
open my mouth.
I drink from the waterfall.

Thirst quenched,
I'm now a squatting lion.
My mane is in corn rolls
made of stone.

My prey is clay figurines
of deer in a frozen leap.

The Undefeated

... The opposite of which
we don't need to go into.
But we will. We will! We have to.

Without these measures
we would not recognize the cricket-sound
of summer heat.
The village fiddler would begin
to dance self-consciously.

The sacred pillar of fire
would burn out
before the party starts.
We need that motley crew
of donkey-faced men.
We need to see them coming
along the road beating tin cans.
People in the crowd
ringing cowbells.

Chanting
in a language we don't know.
Death escorting an old lady
across the street.
And down at the arena
two dead horses.
The opposite of which
we won't go into!

He's watched over
by an undefeated bull.
Wearing a rose
a clown beating a drum.
Striking a pose, the carnival barker

barking at the crowd.
Who says the fading flower
is less lovely
than the one blooming?

The Cycle

Grandpa in the casket
in the living room.
For me, that early experience
made death natural.

Snow and ice melting,
sliding into the river.

In the fireplace
flames reached out
like naked tree limbs.

Pasture fences falling down,
rotting from age.

Then spring, and yellow tulips
and splotches of red.

Spring and a lone man
in a green jacket
on the squeaking planks
looking down upon the water
as if longing for the impossible.

The train going through
the middle of town,
in the middle of the night,

shaking the old buildings,
its whistle louder than
the loudest dog howling.

At the Market

They are haggling over the price of fruit.
There is an uproar.
People take sides.
The critics of puckish malice
will see how brazen this argument is.
People get on their bandwagons.
The seller and the buyer both
are susceptible to shouting.
It's obligatory that I tell the truth:
The argument is bogus—a waste
of everybody's time.
It should never have started.
It started about three pennies.
I once read a retrospective on pennies.
It was a milestone.
The scholar's argument began
from the assumption that the blurry beginnings
of money correlated
with the beginnings of civil conflict
and here we were still at it.

Catharsis

I now forego orthodox techniques.
I purge myself.
I walked through flames to get here.
All my inevitable differences and similarities
melted into one open secret.
They ran the gamut.
I now swim below the icy surface.
I no longer think of the anthropic principle.
Nor natural selection.
Nor the statistical improbability of it all.
Nor the mutational process.
Nor biological adaptation.
Pleasure overcame pain.
With a feathery touch,
I count now my relevant tropes.

Tour de France

At an intersection
we wait with the motor running
as they pass swiftly blurred together.
Boisterous support from the sidelines!
As bikers approach the local finish,
the crowd will cheer and shout and jump out in the road,
and shake their flags in front of advancing bikes.
The riders have come across flat roads and cobbled roads,
up steep hills and across tall mountains,
through Brussels and France
crossing Nancy and Toulouse
and so many other villages and towns.
They've had flat tires, withdrawals, and accidents.
Bystanders will be dying to participate,
to feel the thrill by acclamation.
Consequences matter to them, to us all.
The day is top-heavy, loaded with painful joy.
Jubilant shouts of understanding!
This is just one leg as we wait for them to pass
and victory in Paris is days away.

Sheer Bliss

They say rain is coming in a few hours.
Opaque skies, but beyond lies the sun.
Rattling and grumbling of thunder.
We're under an embroidery of dark clouds.
The day's disquiet sleeps on, dreamless,
melancholy, and indifferent to our wishes.
Our trees, beyond the window, shake,
turning brown, greenish brown.
Looking up to the gray sky,
I'm once again waiting to hear good news.
Any good news! You name it!
Across the street our neighbor
is having a swimming pool installed.
Erratic noise and a lolling all day.
Even in here at my desk,
my private idyll remains out of reach.

Slow Dance

In church grandma did a slow dance.
Her eyes and her skin remembered
centuries of black brown and white bodies
on rotundas handled by the calloused
hands of rude sellers of men and women.
Sugarcane cutters and cotton pickers.
Work songs found their flesh to save them
and they saved the songs too to carry on.
In statehouses and in courthouses
ancestors' plight debated and delayed
for centuries. Mother's mother danced
in church-light to music centuries free
with old cries of liberties. Iron shackles
could not hold the music in check. Her feet
knew the dance before she was born;
and all the world knows it instinctively.

The Trip

Antoinette said
I know a little out-of-the-way restaurant in a village
where the diners are farmers who work with their hands
and wear clothes of blue-cotton comfort.

The food is served on long tables, she said,
and everybody sits together on benches, side by side,
and fill their plates from large pots and bowls

placed in a row before them.
They eat and talk together about their work and their lives.
I think you will enjoy the train ride, especially

as we cross the old railway viaduct into the village.
As we approach, you will see the village
perched up on the rocky spur of the plateau.

If the weather holds, and it's as clear as today,
if from the train window you look down,
you will see the river and the valley.

When we enter and sit among them,
they will look at us curiously, but never mind that.
In time they will warm to our presence.

Irish Nell

In Colonial Chesapeake, Lord Baltimore in 1681
said to his servant Nell don't you know
that if you marry a slave you will become a slave
and all your children and grandchildren
and great-grandchildren from now on into eternity
will become slaves? Nell said I'd rather marry Charles
than to marry you, Lord Baltimore,
and I would rather sleep with Charles
than with you, Lord Baltimore;
and in that same year with a priest presiding
Nell married Charles and she worked the Boarman fields
alongside Charles and slept with Charles
and they had children one after another
and the years passed, and they grew old together
and people called him Negro Charles and called her Irish Nell
and eventually they both died;
but many years later people said
there is nothing in Chesapeake law
saying an Irish woman marrying a slave becomes a slave,
so Irish Nell became White Nell
and her children and grandchildren
and great-grandchildren were set free.

Brooklyn Bridge

Over the East River in the name of Roebling
and sand hogs deep in chambers,
for the first time,
like a friendly hand at the end of a long strong arm,
reaching out to a friend on the other side of a gorge,
the suspension network of steel wires, cables, caissons,
spanning and connecting the two sides,
ending in a magnificent arc.
Stone columns set deep in boxes in the River,
men scooping out bottom-rock and bottom-sand,
all to the glory of the edifice to come.
One side Manhattan, the other Brooklyn,
one rich and dense, the other sparse, a wilderness,
one to the other now no longer the other.
The chasm overcome and Whitman declares, "The best
most effective medicine my soul has yet partaken . . .
the future shall join in one city" the two.
The link, the bridge, Crane's visionary bridge
in exaltation, "night lifted in thine arms."
Boundaries erased, space expanded metaphysically,
in sunrise and in sunset, in rain, snow, and sleet.
Jack's blues in that crossing
and Marianne's "art," and what a fabulous art it is.

Mount Rushmore

We're about thirty miles outside Rapid City, South Dakota,
at Keystone's Black Hills or call it Lakota Paha Sapa.
We're here for Borglum's big faces.
They're granite and longstanding under the sun.
They're sun-baked and whipped by rain
and loved by tourists.

George gazes into an endless distance.
Tom's sight is set high, bravely staring down the light.
Teddy's in somber introspection
and Abe's in a trance.

Is George daydreaming his youth at Pope's Creek
or age eleven getting his first slave,
a man called Trumbull or is George daydreaming
the comforts of Mount Vernon
or the future of America?

Is Tom remembering the importance of dissent
or the frail nature of democracy
(Benjamin's "if you can keep it")
or the swish of Sally Hemings's dress hem
or of Easton's freedom
or is he daydreaming Shadwell's countryside
or the future of humanity?

Is Teddy riding roughly, galloping really,
or thinking about his parks
or a Square Deal for everybody
or railroads or the future of Nature?

Is Abe remembering that first telegraph
or his boat and its title or wrestling days
or the new secret service or is he thinking
about the future of Africans in America
and the future of America?

The Metropolitan Museum of Art

At the Met
you enter not with a bleeding but an open heart,
a heart proudly exposed
like those of ancient saints seriously displaying theirs so
beautifully
on the outside of their blue and red garments,
garments of bright colors
trimmed with yellow gold leaf and sewn with glowing silver thread.
Inside the museum a surprisingly orange-pink mountain rises up
out of a dark thicket of young saplings,
a lonely lady at a table by a window writing a letter,
an ancient Egyptian king sits patiently in a near-empty room.
Bright sunlight splashes down through great windows
into the entryway where thousands enter to the warmth.
That same sunlight shines across vast fields of sunflowers.
Two diggers dig the earth somewhere north of your memory.
Dark skaters in winter's death
with their hands clasped behind their backs
skate quickly and silently across blue ice.
A shopgirl walks to market carrying a straw basket.
An ox pulls a clunky wagon across a shaky drawbridge.
You gaze knowingly under clouds at a rocky cliffside.
A woman in a long black dress and white shawl of lace
sits in a straw chair by a table knitting a scarf
for the coming winter months.
The wooden boat-people arriving naked and desperate for help.
A Dutch girl stands by her grandmother's kitchen window
pouring water from a silver pitcher into an ornate bowl.
A wooden ceremonial figure speaks of its journey
from deep in the jungles of Peru;
and you turn slowly and look back
at everything you've seen and gleaned
and you discover parts of yourself in each of them.

The Statue of Liberty

More Roman thank Greek
her arm raised holding a cup of light,
lighting the way, some say all the way.
Bartholdi's colossal, a framed idea in metal
by Eiffel singing layers of garment, greened
by weather; an 1886 symbol of liberty
and independence seen from sunup till sundown
through clouds fog snow and rain
and even in lighted darkness glowing
for a long distance a goddess carrying a reminder
of that declaration taken and too often forgotten,
but not forgotten is the giver's message of freedom.

Island of the Pelicans

First I saw the movie *Birdman of Alcatraz*
with Burt Lancaster as Robert Shroud,
then from the city the actual Rock.

About eighty years after Ayala
named the city in stress
to protect from invaders from betrayers,
they built a fortress on the rock
but warriors nor renegades came
so they thought to convert the fortress
to warehouse prisoners of war.

With no prisoners of war,
at gunpoint they forced convicts
to convert the fortress to a prison,
rock by rock, stone by stone, slab by slab,
they were shut in.

Later, Robert Shroud, also shut in.
He read everything on birds he could find,
becoming an expert.
When they took away his birds
he wrote a book on bird diseases.

The movie version shows us a gentle Shroud,
not a vicious killer, Lancaster soft-spoken,
who happens to care for birds, especially canaries.
For me Lancaster, not Shroud, is Bird Man.

The Grand Canyon

Thirsty, I stop at Pima Point to look down
at the Colorado River,
at two billion years of geological history,
five million years running, now
in this moment pink reflected sunlight,
deep in its rugged crevice bed.
Under both sun and haze,
Boucher Rapids, Crystal Creek, Tuna Creek, Scorpion Ridge.

This is land of ancient Pueblo people,
Hopi and Navajo. I marvel at the canyon
where cliffs, tributaries, caves, plateau
lift and curve and cut and drop and rise.
Thirst quenched, I drive on east
with the canyon inside to stay forever.

Las Vegas Strip

In a crowed elevator
in a Vegas casino,
a drunk cowboy in a ten-gallon hat
and pink cowboy boots,
says, *I wish I was in Texas,*
and a few of us laugh,
but he turns to me with a menacing look
and says, *Did I say something funny?*
His friend says, *Let it go, Teddy.*
I'd already lost some money
and this made me feel worse, but

still I had an interest in Vegas.
Highway 91 and the Strip were jumping.
I knew the history. If you were white,
back in '31 you could get lucky
with a pair of dice at the Pair-o-Dice.
All you had to do was throw the dice.

There Sammy couldn't stay,
Sammy couldn't eat, Sammy couldn't gamble,
but he and his daddy could entertain them.
So could Duke with his big band,
but he couldn't stay or eat or gamble.

We got into the war in '41 and
El Rancho Vegas threw open its doors,
and the Strip was born—the Riviera,
Caesars, the Nugget, you name it.
In the '40s and '50s
Bugsy had Spike or Satchmo or the Stooges.

The Strip dimmed the lights when
Elvis and Sammy and Dean and Sinatra
flew off to the stars becoming light.

The Birth of Times Square

Muddy road with carriages,
Street sweepers sweeping droppings.
Burlesque house. Hotel Cadillac. Astor Theatre.
Proper ladies in long white dresses
holding onto their bonnets and parasols.
Mr. Ochs' spanking new skyscraper.
Longacre becoming Times Square.
Wave to Apparel for Women.
Bond's two-trouser suits.
Bright lights, bustling Square.
Yellow cabs, bumper to bumper.
Kodak and Coca-Cola.
Above it all, a thin slice of sky
of comfort and reassurance.

CPSIA information can be obtained
at www.ICGtesting.com
Printed in the USA
LVHW051540230422
717055LV00007B/283

9 780807 176108